SATOMI ICHIKAWA

Rosy's Garden

A CHILD'S KEEPSAKE

OF FLOWERS

Text copyright © 1990 by Elizabeth Laird.
Illustrations copyright © 1990 by Satomi Ichikawa.
Published by Philomel Books,
a division of The Putnam & Grosset Group,
200 Madison Avenue, New York, NY 10016.
All rights reserved.
First American Edition 1990.
Printed in Hong Kong.

Library of Congress Cataloging-in-Publication Data
Laird, Elizabeth.   Rosy's garden.
SUMMARY: Visiting her grandmother in the country,
Rosy learns facts and folklore about flowers as she
presses flowers, gathers seeds, and makes potpourri.
1. Flowers – Juvenile literature.   2. Flower gardening –
Juvenile literature.   3. Flowers – Folklore – Juvenile
literature.   4. Flowers – Utilization – Juvenile
literature.   5. Herbs – Juvenile literature.
[1. Flowers. 2. Flowers – Folklore. 3. Gardening]
I. Ichikawa, Satomi, ill.   II. Title.
SB406.5.L35   1990   635.9   89-22955
ISBN 0-399-21881-5

Satomi Ichikawa

Rosy's Garden

A CHILD'S KEEPSAKE
OF FLOWERS

Text by Elizabeth Laird

PHILOMEL BOOKS

NEW YORK

For Stella and Jessie, with love

S.I.

For my Mother

E.L.

The kiss of the sun for pardon,
The song of the birds for mirth,
One is nearer God's heart in a garden
Than anywhere else on earth.

Dorothy Frances Gurney

Contents

A Welcome for Rosy

"Rosy!" says Granny happily. "You're here at last!"
Rosy skips into Granny's kitchen, and looks around. It's lovely – just as she remembers it. There are flowers everywhere, a jug of irises on the table, honeysuckle on the wallpaper, and crocus growing in pots on the windowsill. There are other interesting things on the windowsill too.

"What are those little plants?" says Rosy.

"More flowers." Granny smiles. "Pansies, and sweet williams, and petunias . . ."

"But there aren't any flowers on them," says Rosy.

"There will be soon," says Granny. "I'm going to plant them out in the garden tomorrow. Then they'll grow very fast."

"Can I help?" says Rosy. "I love gardening."

"Of course you can," says Granny. "You can be my Chief Assistant. I've got a special trowel and fork, just for you to use."

"But will the flowers come out before I have to go home?" says Rosy.

"Yes," says Granny. "Mother says you can stay for the whole summer if you want to."

"Oh, I do want to!" says Rosy, "I do!"

Then she notices something she has never seen before. Around Granny's neck is a locket. Rosy opens it. Inside are some little purple violets, rather faded, but still pretty.

"Where do these come from?" asks Rosy.

"It's a long story," says Granny. "Let me make myself a cup of tea, and I'll tell you all about it."

A Gift of Violets

"My big brother Tom could run so fast, and climb so high, and scramble so quickly over fences that I could never catch up with him," Granny says. "Well, one lovely spring day, when I was six or seven years old, Mother said we could go into the woods to look for primroses, but when we got halfway there, Tom met his best friend.

"I've seen some baby thrushes in a nest," he said. "Come along, I'll show you."

"They ran off, and left me all alone, in the woods!"

"What did you do?" asks Rosy.

"I called out, and no one answered, so I sat down on a tree stump and cried."

"That's what I'd have done," says Rosy.

"But crying doesn't get you anywhere," says Granny, "so after a while I got up, and looked for a path, and at last I found my way home. The boys stayed out all day, looking for birds' nests. They even forgot to come home for tea."

"Was your mother cross?" asks Rosy.

"Yes," says Granny, "and so was I, but not for long, because the next day Tom's friend waited for me all morning in the garden, and when I came out in the afternoon, he gave me a bunch of violets, and said he was very sorry, and he'd never be horrid to me again."

"And was he?" says Rosy.

"No," says Granny. "Edward was the kindest man I ever knew."

"Edward?" says Rosy. "But that was Grandfather's name!"

"Yes, dear," says Granny, "and these are Edward's violets." And she carefully shuts the locket.

Granny's Garden

Outside, in the garden, Rosy runs up
one path and down another.

"It's perfect!" she says. "It's the most
lovely garden I've ever seen! It's the
loveliest garden in the world!"

A Craze for Tulips

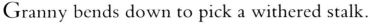

Granny bends down to pick a withered stalk.

"What's that?" asks Rosy.

"It was a tulip," says Granny. "It doesn't look very interesting now, but tulips were once the most precious flowers in the world."

Tulips did not grow wild in Europe. They came from Turkey, nearly four hundred years ago. They were rare, and special, and everyone loved them for their bright colors, and because they sometimes had stripes in brilliant shades of red, pink, orange, yellow and white.

In Holland in 1634, there was a mad craze for tulips. People would pay thousands of florins for tulip plants. Some even sold their houses and all their land for just one bulb. They hoped to plant it, and produce more bulbs from it, which they could sell for even more money.

Not everyone made money out of tulips. One tulip farmer sat down to supper one night to enjoy his usual stew. It tasted unusual.

"What did you put in it?" he asked his cook.

"Oh, nothing special," said the cook. "Just onions and meat."

"Show me the onions," said the farmer.

The cook showed him what he had used, and the farmer went mad with rage.

"You fool!" he yelled. "You've cooked my best tulip bulbs instead of onions! My supper has cost me 100,000 florins!"

The tulip craze only lasted for a few years, but Dutch people still love them. Every spring, the tulip fields of Holland are covered with miles of beautiful, brilliant flowers, and the Dutch farmers send out their bulbs to bloom in every corner of the world.

Old Names for Old Flowers

"I wish I knew what all the flowers are called," says Rosy.

"You'll soon learn their names," says Granny, "and very ancient some of them are too. Some are even in a poem that's nearly six hundred years old.

> Periwinkle, violet, cowslip and lily,
> Rose red, rose white, foxglove and primrose,
> Hollyhock, coriander, peony . . ."

"It doesn't really sound like a poem," says Rosy. "It doesn't rhyme."

"No, it doesn't," says Granny. "You'd better make up another one when you know all the flower names yourself."

CARNATION
These flowers were greatly loved in the Middle Ages. They were often used to make garlands and coronets, and came to be called 'coronation,' or 'carnation.'

LILY
Old painters loved this flower and often painted the Virgin Mary with lilies, so that it became the symbol of all that is good and beautiful.

DELPHINIUM
The Greeks thought the buds of this flower looked like dolphins so they called it 'delphinos,' which is Greek for dolphin. Delphinium comes from 'delphinos.'

HOLLYHOCK
The Crusaders probably brought this flower to Europe from its home in the East. They used to make the flowers into a kind of tea and drink it when they had a bad cold.

POPPY
In the First World War, a Canadian poet, John McCrae, wrote a famous poem about the poppies that grew in the fields of Flanders, where many soldiers died. Soon people started wearing poppies in honor of fallen soldiers.

HONEYSUCKLE
Perhaps it is the sweet smell of honeysuckle that makes it so romantic. There's an old superstition that if you bring honeysuckle into the house a wedding will follow.

Lilies of the Valley

Near the lavender bush in Granny's garden, there's a shy little plant with an even stronger smell. Little white bells hanging from a stalk peep out from its long, pointed leaves.

"I know what that is," says Rosy, sniffing the air. "Mother has some scent like that in a pretty glass bottle. It's lily of the valley, isn't it, Granny?"

"That's right," says Granny. "The Germans call it 'little bells of May', and the French even have a special day for it. They think it brings good luck."

"What do they do?" asks Rosy.

"On the first of May every year," says Granny, "the streets of French towns and villages are full of the lovely scent of lily of the valley. There are people selling it at every corner, and everyone buys bunches of it to give to their friends. The shops make special displays. Bakers make cakes with iced lily of the valley on them, and sweetsellers sell green and white sweets."

"How lovely!" says Rosy. "What about the children? What do they do?"

"They pick big bunches of them," says Granny, "or buy them from a flower seller, and make them into bouquets. Then they give them to older friends, perhaps to their neighbors, or their aunts, or . . ."

She stops. While she has been talking, Rosy has been busy. She has picked a bunch of the delicate white flowers and now she gives it to Granny.

". . . Or to their grandmothers!" finishes Granny with a smile.

Lavender Blue, Lavender Green

Rosy runs down a little stone path and brushes against a grey-green bush with small blue flowers.

"I know this one!" she says. "It's lavender! I know a song about it, too."

"Go on then," says Granny. "Sing it to me."

Lavender's blue, diddle diddle,
Lavender's green;
When I am king, diddle diddle,
You shall be queen.

Roses are red, diddle diddle,
Violets are blue;
Because you love me, diddle diddle,
I will love you.

Who told you so, diddle, diddle,
Who told you so?
'Twas mine own heart, diddle, diddle,
That told me so.

"I used to sing that when I was your age," says Granny.

"Did you really?"

"Yes," says Granny, "and I did something else too. I used to sew little muslin bags and fill them with dried lavender flowers, then I'd tuck them in with my handkerchieves and clothes. They made everything smell lovely."

"Let's pick some lavender flowers, Granny, so that I can make a bag and take it home."

The Children of the Sky

"Do all the flowers have stories?" asks Rosy.

"Most do," says Granny.

"What's the nicest of them all?"

"I like the one about the forget-me-not best," says Granny.

In the morning of the world, an angel flew out of the gates of Heaven. He was taking a message to a holy man who lived in the Persian desert. But as he flew through the air, the angel saw a beautiful Persian girl sitting by a well, weaving forget-me-nots into her hair. The angel landed at her side, and looked into her eyes, and forgot everything except how beautiful she was.

"I love you," he said, and the girl smiled.

So the girl and the angel got married, and lived happily together, but one day the angel remembered his message, and, with his wife, he flew back to heaven to ask for pardon. But when he got there he found the gates of heaven closed against them, and the Archangel Gabriel standing on guard.

"What are you thinking of?" said Gabriel. "You cannot bring a daughter of earth into heaven!" The angel wept in anguish, and Gabriel was sorry for him.

"First go, and cover the earth with the children of the sky," he said, "and then you can bring her in."

The angel did not understand, but the girl did. She took the forget-me-nots from her hair, and she and her husband wandered through the world, planting them. And when the forget-me-nots flowered, and the earth was as blue as the sky, the angel picked up his bride, and flew with her in through the gates of heaven.

Flower Names

"I especially like roses," says Rosy, "because of my name."

"I've got a flower name, too," says Granny.

"No, you haven't," says Rosy. "Your name's Margaret."

"Yes," says Granny, "but in French it's 'Marguerite,' and that means 'Daisy.' Everyone used to call me Daisy when I was little."

"Are there lots of flower names?" says Rosy.

"Yes," says Granny, "and tree names, too."

TREE NAMES	FLOWER NAMES
Hazel	Heather
Olivia and Olive	Iris
Holly	Lily
Daphne	Marigold
	Poppy

The Language of Flowers

"Did you know," says Granny, "that many flowers have a special meaning? In the old days, you had to be careful when you gave someone a posy of flowers. If they knew the language of flowers, they might think you were trying to give them a secret message. Red chrysanthemums meant 'I love,' and four-leaf clover meant 'Be mine.' But hydrangeas meant 'Heartless' and Michaelmas daisies meant 'Goodbye.'"

SOME FLOWER MEANINGS

Anemone – *forsaken*
Bluebell – *constancy*
Red carnation – *alas for my poor heart!*
Columbine – *folly*
Cowslip – *thoughtfulness*
Daisy – *innocence*
Forget-me-not – *true love*
French marigold – *jealousy*
Hyacinth – *sport or game*
Lavender – *distrust*
Lily – *purity, sweetness*
Lily of the valley – *return of happiness*

Marigold – *grief*
Orange blossom – *purity, loveliness*
Pansy – *thoughts*
Rose – *love*
Rosemary – *remembrance*
Snowdrop – *hope*
Violet – *modesty*
Yew – *sorrow*

Fairy Dreams

The summer days pass quickly in Granny's garden. Stiff lupin spikes are standing in the flower bed, and the rosebuds are beginning to open. Soon the air is full of the scent of honeysuckle. It comes from Rosy's favorite part of the garden, an old summer house in a sleepy corner, almost smothered with creamy, pale-yellow flowers. Rosy likes to come here with a book and an apple on hot, lazy afternoons, and hear the bees, and as she curls up in her favorite chair, she murmurs a little poem to herself.

Honeysuckle, twisting, climbing
Round and over, up and down.
Every flower a Sleeping Beauty
In a lacy dressing gown.

Honeysuckle, heavy-scented,
On a lazy summer's day,
Yawning, nodding, eyelids closing,
Dreaming quiet hours away.

And when Rosy is fast asleep, who knows what little visitors might come and play around her?

Rose Poems

O, my Luve's like a red red rose
That's newly sprung in June:
O my Luve's like the melodie
That's sweetly played in tune.

Robert Burns

Queen rose of the rosebud garden of girls
Come hither, the dances are done,
In gloss of satin and shimmer of pearls,
Queen lily and rose in one;
Shine out, little head, sunning over with curls,
To the flowers, and be their sun.

Lord Tennyson

Gather ye rosebuds while ye may,
Old Time is still a-flying:
And this same flower that smiles today,
Tomorrow will be dying.

Robert Herrick

I know a bank whereon the wild thyme blows
Where oxlips and the nodding violet grows;
Quite o'er canopied with luscious woodbine
With sweet musk-roses, and with eglantine:
There sleeps Titania, sometime of the night
Lull'd in these flowers, with dances and delight.

William Shakespeare

There is a garden in her face
Where roses and white lilies grow
A heav'nly paradise is that place,
Wherein all pleasant fruits do flow.
There cherries grow, which none may buy,
Till 'Cherry ripe' themselves do cry.

Thomas Campion

Rosy Things

Rosy loves to cup the sweet-smelling dark red roses in her hands, and breathe in their perfume.

"It's a pity they don't grow all the year around," she says. "It would be nice to smell them in the winter, too."

"But you can," says Granny. "You can make rose water, and face lotion, and pot-pourri and . . ."

"Oh, show me how," says Rosy. "Please, Granny."

ROSE WATER

- Fill a saucepan with the petals from strongly scented red roses.
- Add enough water to cover.
- Bring to the boil and simmer for a few minutes.
- Allow to cool, keeping the lid on to keep the perfume in.
- Strain into jars with good stoppers, or bottles with screw-on caps.
- Use rose water as a delicate perfume on your skin, or sprinkle a little on your clothes.

POT-POURRI

Dry rose petals and lavender flowers for two or three weeks on trays in a warm, airy place away from sunlight. Turn them daily to prevent mildew.

Mix together in a bowl 4 oz rose petals, 2 oz lavender, a teaspoon each of dried marjoram, rosemary and crushed cloves. Add 5 drops of rose oil and 3 drops of lavender oil.

Put the pot-pourri into a large plastic bag and seal it tightly. Leave it for a few weeks to mature, shaking well every other day.

Pot-pourri can either be used to stuff pretty bags made of cotton or silk, or left in bowls to perfume a room.

FACE LOTION

3 tablespoons glycerine
4 tablespoons rose water

- Put both glycerine and rose water into a bottle with a screw-on cap.
- Shake them together until they are properly mixed.

Cherry Ripe!

The cherries are ripe at last! Rosy and Granny have to pick them before the birds get them all.

"Why aren't there any cherries on the other tree?" asks Rosy.

"It's a flowering cherry," says Granny. "It has flowers, but no fruit."

"How silly," says Rosy. "I wouldn't want a cherry tree that didn't have any cherries."

"Oh yes, you would," says Granny. "Every spring the flowering cherry has so many flowers you can hardly see the branches. And when the petals fall, they cover the grass like pink snow. In Japan, people love the flowering cherries so much they have special cherry tree gardens, and festivals to celebrate the time when they flower. They put a red cloth out on the ground, and have a picnic."

Loveliest of trees, the cherry now
Is hung with bloom along the bough,
And stands about the woodland ride
Wearing white for Eastertide.

A. E. Housman

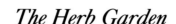

The Herb Garden

There's a corner of Granny's garden where only herbs are allowed to grow. Rosy knows all their names. "Rosemary, thyme, mint, parsley, sage . . ." she says, as she picks a leaf off each plant and crushes them in her fingers. The rich, herby smells make her think of times long ago, when medieval ladies grew herbs in between neat little paths in the castle gardens, and strewed herbs on the floor to make the great hall smell sweet, and when they made medicines and ointments out of herbs, to cure everything from headaches to bee stings.

And where the marjoram once, and sage
and rue
And balm and mint, with curled-leaved
parsley grew,
And double marigold, and silver thyme,
And pumpkins 'neath the window used
to climb;
And where I often, when a child, for hours,
Tried through the pales to get the tempting
flowers.

John Clare

pales – wooden fence

Herby Things

Granny knows lots of interesting things to do with herbs. She and Rosy try some of them out together.

AN HERBAL BATH

Chop up a cupful of rosemary leaves and lavender leaves. Put them in a saucepan and cover with a pint of water. Cover, bring to the boil, and simmer for thirty minutes. Leave to cool, keeping the lid of the saucepan on so that the smell does not escape. Strain into a jar and keep it in the bathroom. Add a cupful of the liquid to make a refreshing, sweet-smelling bath.

AN HERBY SANDWICH

brown bread or roll
cream cheese
chives, mint and parsley

Chop together chives, mint and parsley, mix well with the cream cheese and spread it on your bread or roll to make a delicious sandwich.

A MINTY SALAD

half a cucumber
a pint of yogurt
half a cup of chopped mint

Chop up the cucumber and stir in the yogurt and mint. This makes a lovely cool salad on a hot day.

HERBY RICE
8 oz long grain rice
1 pint of water
a stick of butter
a few slices of onion
a cup of chopped herbs, parsley,
mint, thyme, marjoram

Boil the rice and water together until the
water has all disappeared, and the grains of
rice are soft and fluffy (about 15 minutes).
Stir in the butter, and onion chopped very
small, and the herbs. This goes very well
with any meat or fish dish.

The Bright Flowers of Spain

The postman's brought a card for Rosy. It's from her friend, Emily, who is on holiday in Spain. Rosy's been to Spain. She went with her parents last year. They rented a little house near the sea, and Rosy went swimming every day in the warm water.

The flowers in their little Spanish garden were quite different from Granny's flowers. They were bigger, and bolder, and brighter. There are some Spanish flowers on Emily's card. Rosy remembers their names.

"Look, Granny," she says, "this little fluffy yellow one that grows on trees is mimosa. It makes you sneeze if you get too close to it. And these big red trumpets are hibiscus, and this spiky, prickly thing's a yucca, and this pink one's an oleander, and oh, that's all."

"Not quite," says Granny. "You've missed that little shrub in the corner. It's a laurel, and it's got an interesting story."

In ancient times a river god had a beautiful daughter called Daphne. She was a great huntress and did not want to get married. One day, the god Apollo saw her and fell in love with her. Daphne ran away, but the god chased her and nearly caught her.

"Father! Save me!" called Daphne.

The river god heard his daughter. Quickly, he changed her into a tree. Her feet became roots, her arms branches, and her hair leaves.

Apollo never forgot Daphne. He wove her leaves into a wreath and always wore a crown of laurels.

The Wild Flowers of Summer

At the bottom of Granny's garden a stream runs through a
meadow, bright with summer flowers. Buttercups and daisies,
meadowsweet and clover, ladies' smocks and dandelions all
grow there. The smallest flowers are the loveliest of all,
sky-blue speedwell, star-like scarlet pimpernel,
and yellow birds' foot trefoil.

Flowery Games

Rosy picks a dandelion and blows on it. After four puffs all the seeds have blown away.

"It must be four o'clock," says Rosy.

"Nearly tea-time," says Granny.

She picks a buttercup and holds it under Rosy's chin. Her skin shines golden yellow.

"You *do* like butter," she says. "I thought so."

Rosy picks a daisy and pulls off the petals one by one.

"She loves me, she loves me not, she loves me," she says.

In the end, only one petal is left.

"She loves me!" says Rosy.

"Who does?" asks Granny.

"You do," says Rosy, and she skips off down the path.

"Pick me some more flowers," says Granny, "and I'll show you what we can do with them."

Rosy has picked a dandelion, a daisy, and a speedwell. She presses them between sheets of newspaper and leaves them under a stack of heavy books. In a week or two they'll be dry and flat, and Rosy will be able to use them. She'll stick one at the top of a letter to Mother.

"Let's make some lavender notepaper," says Granny. "It smells lovely. Then when you write to Mother, she'll be able to smell the garden herself."

"How do you do it?" says Rosy.

"It's easy," says Granny.

LAVENDER NOTEPAPER

- Cut lavender heads just before the flowers open.
- Tie them in bunches and hang them away from the sun in a warm, dry, airy room.
- When they are dry, shake off all the flowers.
- Put handfuls of flowers into two or three envelopes, and seal them.
- Tuck the envelopes among your notepaper.
- Keep your notepaper in a box with a lid, so that the lavender smell does not waft away.

Shy Flowers from the Mountains

Granny's busy, too. She's adding a few more embroidered flowers to Rosy's summer blouse. She does them in easy satin stitches in brightly-colored threads.

Rosy looks like a little girl from the mountains in her embroidered blouse. It's covered with the bright little flowers that grow in the Alpine meadows. There are cornflowers, and jonquils, deep blue gentians, and the little white edelweiss. Once, so a Swiss legend says, the edelweiss was a beautiful maiden who died unmarried, and still lives on, high in the mountains, among the ice and snow, as a shy little flower.

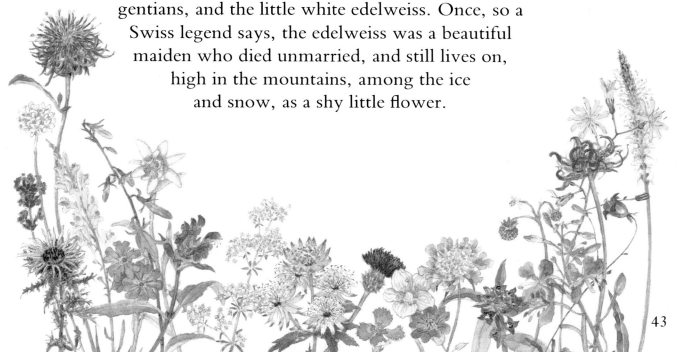

Seed Time

It's late summer now, but Granny and Rosy still have plenty of work to do. They've collected a lot of seeds, and now they carefully store them in envelopes, ready to plant next year.

"How will they know when to start growing?" says Rosy.

"That's one of nature's secrets," says Granny. "The more you know about old Mother Nature, the more you see how wonderful she is."

A Last Bouquet

It's Rosy's last morning in the country, and she's got a surprise for Granny.

"Do you remember that poem," she says, "the old one about flowers that didn't really rhyme? Well, I've made up another one.

> Larkspur and honeysuckle
> Candytuft and rose,
> In Granny's garden
> Everything grows.
>
> Hollyhock, lavender,
> Snapdragon too,
> Rosemary, thyme
> And forget-me-not blue.'

"Well done!" says Granny.
"There's a bit more," says Rosy.

> "Please Granny, please Granny,
> Please Granny dear,
> Please may I, please may I
> Come back next year?"

"Of course you can," says Granny, "but before you go home, there's one last job to do. Let's pick a bouquet of all the nicest flowers we can find for Mother. Are you ready, Chief Assistant?"